AMAZING BODY SYST

IMMUNE SYSTEM

by Karen Latchana Kenney

pogo

Ideas for Parents and Teachers

Pogo Books let children practice reading informational text while introducing them to nonfiction features such as headings, labels, sidebars, maps, and diagrams, as well as a table of contents, glossary, and index.

Carefully leveled text with a strong photo match offers early fluent readers the support they need to succeed.

Before Reading

- "Walk" through the book and point out the various nonfiction features. Ask the student what purpose each feature serves.
- Look at the glossary together. Read and discuss the words.

Read the Book

- Have the child read the book independently.
- Invite him or her to list questions that arise from reading.

After Reading

- Discuss the child's questions. Talk about how he or she might find answers to those questions.
- Prompt the child to think more. Ask: What other body systems do you know about? What do they do? How might they interact with the immune system?

Pogo Books are published by Jump!
5357 Penn Avenue South
Minneapolis, MN 55419
www.jumplibrary.com

Library of Congress Cataloging-in-Publication Data

Names: Kenney, Karen Latchana, author.
Title: Immune system / by Karen Latchana Kenney.
Description: Minneapolis, MN: Jump!, Inc. [2017]
Series: Amazing body systems | Audience: Ages 7-10.
Includes bibliographical references and index.
Identifiers: LCCN 2016038904 (print)
LCCN 2016039480 (ebook)
ISBN 9781620315569 (hardcover: alk. paper)
ISBN 9781620315989 (pbk.)
ISBN 9781624965043 (ebook)
Subjects: LCSH: Immune system--Juvenile literature.
Classification: LCC QR181.8 .K46 2017 (print)
LCC QR181.8 (ebook) | DDC 616.07/9--dc23
LC record available at https://lccn.loc.gov/2016038904

Series Editor: Jenny Fretland VanVoorst
Series Designer: Anna Peterson
Photo Researcher: Anna Peterson

Photo Credits: All photos by Shutterstock except: Getty, 10-11, 16-17, 18-19; iStock, 5; SuperStock, 14-15, 20-21.

Printed in the United States of America at Corporate Graphics in North Mankato, Minnesota.

TABLE OF CONTENTS

CHAPTER 1

··

YOUR BODY'S ARMY

First you feel a sore throat.
Then you start sneezing.
Soon your whole
head feels
stuffed up.
You have a cold.

You feel bad. But your stuffy head is a good thing. It means your **immune system** is working. It is fighting off the **virus**.

germs

A virus is a kind of **germ**.
Bacteria are another.
Germs attack your cells.
This can make you sick.

The immune system is your body's army. Some parts block germs from coming in. But sometimes they get inside your body. Other parts of the immune system destroy them.

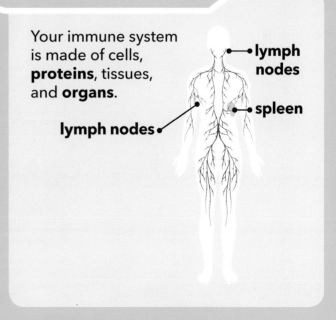

TAKE A LOOK!

Your immune system is made of cells, **proteins**, tissues, and **organs**.

lymph nodes

spleen

lymph nodes

CHAPTER 2

....

BLOCK AND ATTACK

Your skin is your body's biggest germ blocker. It stops many germs from entering your body.

mucus ‧‧‧‧▶

Sticky **mucus** lines the nose, throat, and stomach. It traps germs. Tiny moving hairs push the germs up. A sneeze or cough makes germs fly out.

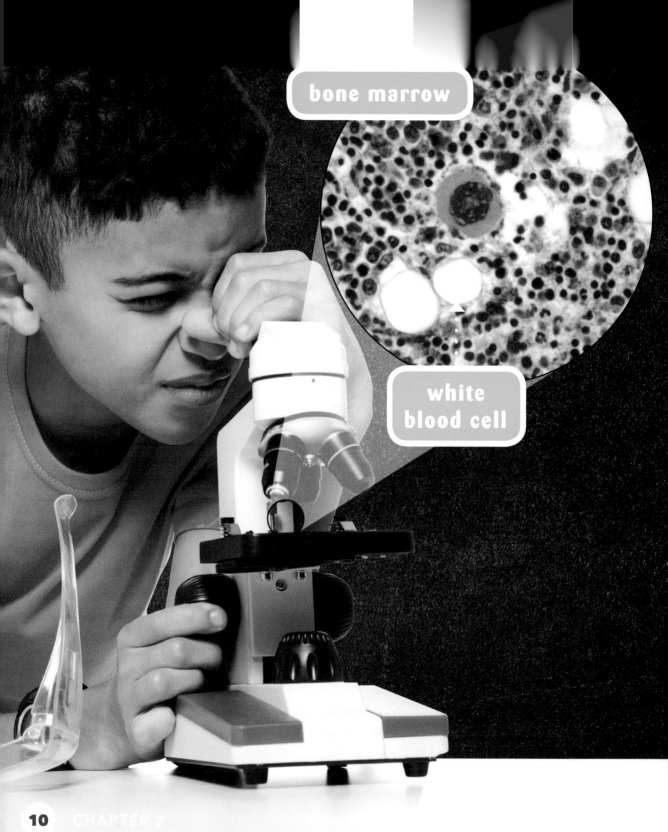

bone marrow

white
blood cell

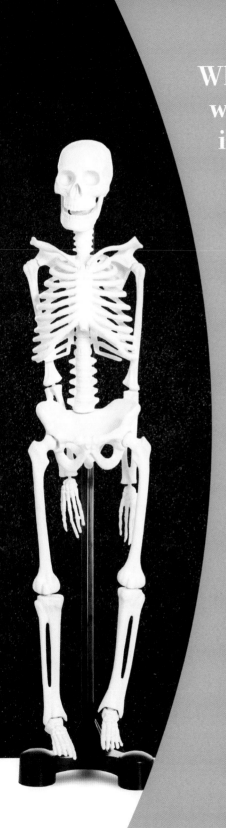

What if germ blockers don't work? Your immune cells step in. These white blood cells are made in **bone marrow**. They move through **blood vessels** to find germs.

THINK ABOUT IT!

You touch a lot of things with your hands. Then you touch your eyes, nose, or mouth. That's how some germs enter the body. So wash your hands!

Different immune cells have different jobs. A **T cell** knows what germ is in the body. It tells other immune cells to attack.

A **B cell** makes a protein called an **antibody**. It is made just for a certain germ. It sticks to the germ. The germ can't grow. Then it dies.

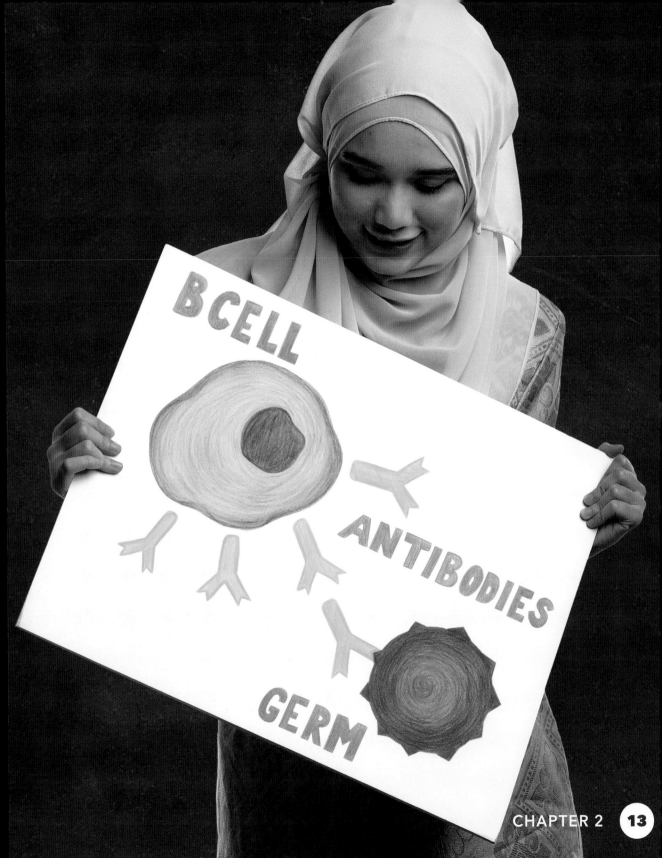

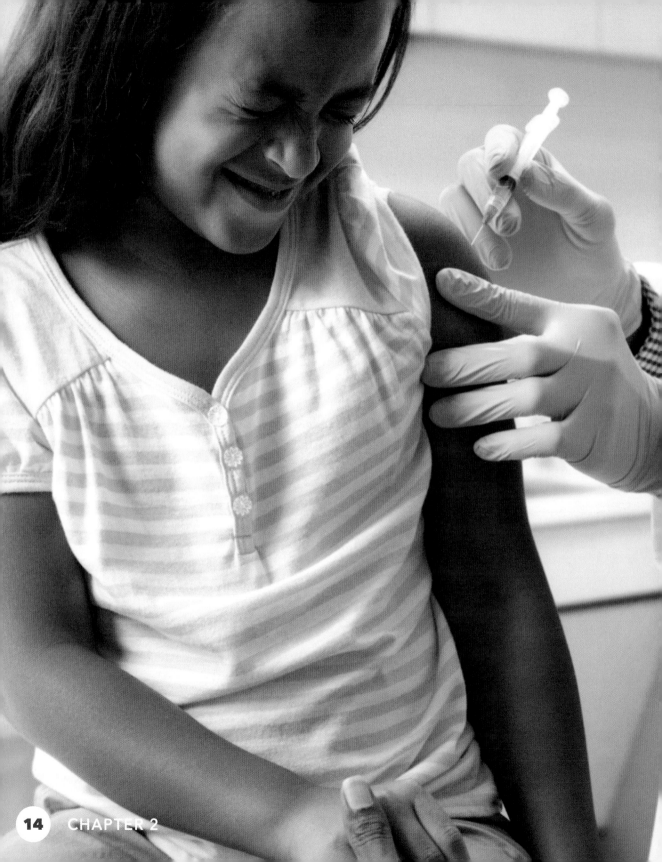

Have you ever gotten a shot to keep you from getting sick? These shots contain small amounts of a germ. It's such a small amount that you don't get sick. But your immune cells will know the germ next time. They will be able to attack more quickly.

CHAPTER 3

CLEAN-UP CREW

You have germ filters in your body, too. Lymph is a clear fluid. It collects germs from your tissues. Then it moves to lymph nodes.

You have thousands of lymph nodes. Some bigger ones are in your neck and armpits. These nodes are packed with immune cells. They remove germs. All clean!

Your **spleen** helps remove germs, too. It is by your stomach. Blood vessels carry blood into the spleen. The organ picks out bad blood cells and germs.

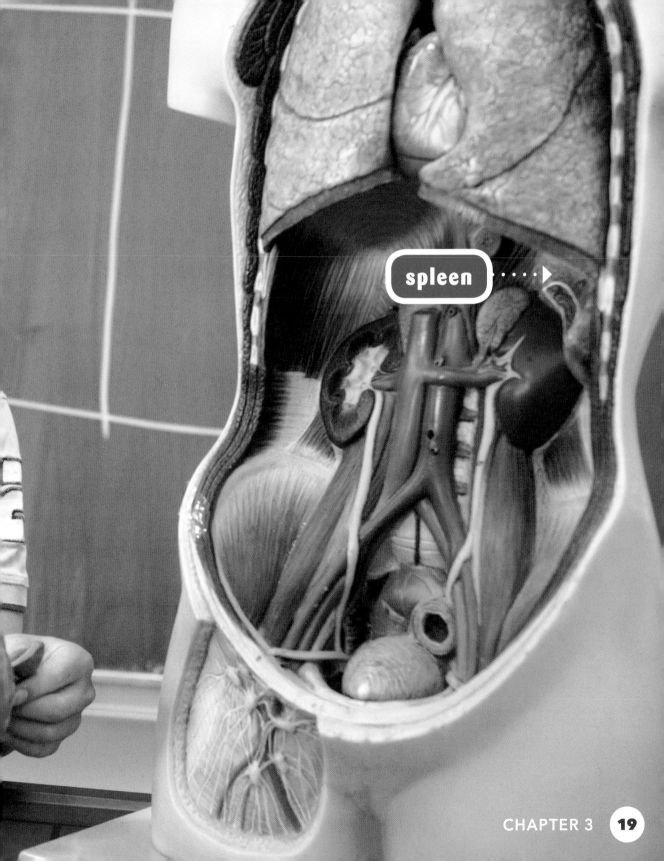

spleen ·····▶

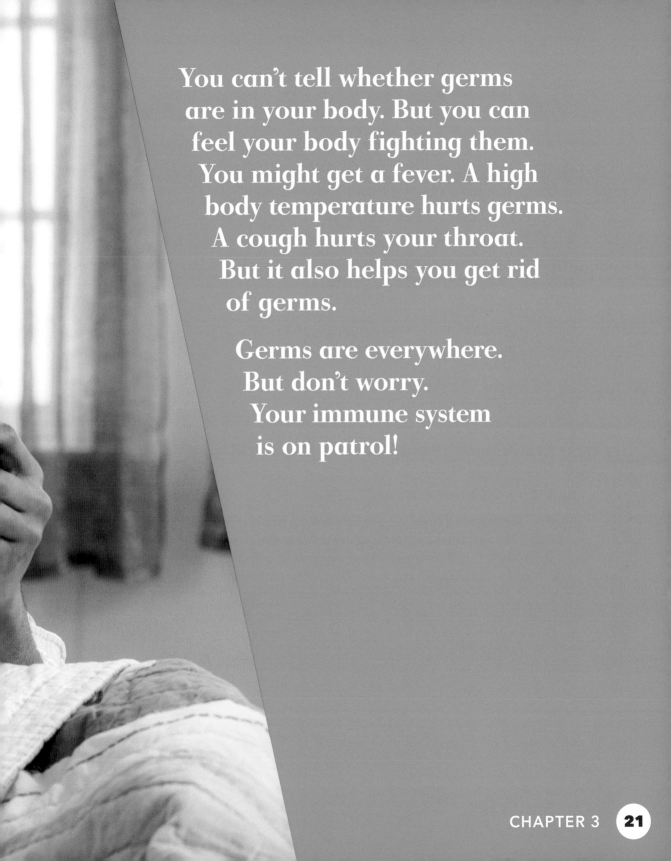

You can't tell whether germs are in your body. But you can feel your body fighting them. You might get a fever. A high body temperature hurts germs. A cough hurts your throat. But it also helps you get rid of germs.

Germs are everywhere. But don't worry. Your immune system is on patrol!

ACTIVITIES & TOOLS

STICKY MUCUS

Try making mucus. Then see if you can figure out how it stops germs.

What You Need:
- 3 packets of unflavored gelatin
- ½ cup of boiling water (ask a parent for help with this)
- 2 bowls
- ½ cup corn syrup
- fork

1 **Put the boiling water in a bowl. Slowly add the gelatin. Mix with a fork.**

2 **Let it sit for five minutes.**

3 **Put the corn syrup in another bowl. Slowly stir in the gelatin mix. This makes the mucus. Feel the mucus with your fingers. What does it feel like? How do you think it stops germs?**

GLOSSARY

antibody: A protein that fights germs.

bacteria: Tiny creatures that live inside and outside of the body.

B cell: A type of white blood cell that circulates in our blood and creates proteins called antibodies that destroy germs.

blood vessels: Tubes that carry blood around the body.

bone marrow: A soft inside layer of bones that makes blood cells and stores fat.

germ: A microscopic living thing that causes disease.

immune system: A body system that protects the body and kills germs.

mucus: A sticky liquid that coats your nose, throat, and mouth.

organs: Parts of the body that do certain jobs.

proteins: Living material found in animal and plant cells.

spleen: An organ that filters blood.

T cell: A type of white blood cell that circulates in our blood and scans for infections.

virus: A tiny creature that enters cells inside the body.

INDEX

TO LEARN MORE

Learning more is as easy as 1, 2, 3.

1) Go to www.factsurfer.com

2) Enter "immunesystem" into the search box.

3) Click the "Surf" button to see a list of websites.

With factsurfer, finding more information is just a click away.